Original title:
Whispers Behind the Window

Copyright © 2025 Creative Arts Management OÜ
All rights reserved.

Author: Lila Davenport
ISBN HARDBACK: 978-1-80587-114-9
ISBN PAPERBACK: 978-1-80587-584-0

Hidden Hopes at Dawn

At dawn, the cat takes flight,
Chasing dreams right out of sight.
Socks are strewn, a fun display,
The shoes are laughing, 'It's our day!'

The toast pops up with a cheer,
While butter's ready, never fear.
Coffee brews its comic tune,
As cereal dances with the spoon.

Linger Long on the Threshold

On the steps, the old frog croaks,
Sharing jokes, a laugh provokes.
Neighbors peek through curtains tight,
To catch the banter, pure delight.

The mailbox winks, it's full of cheer,
With letters that insist, 'Come near!'
But the cat informs, 'Not today,
I'm busy napping in my play.'

The Soft Language of Shadows

Shadows dance upon the wall,
Whispering secrets, big and small.
The lampshade grins, it plays pretend,
While dust bunnies plot to offend.

The chair chuckles, creaks with glee,
As the rug gives a ticklish plea.
Together they weave a jolly tale,
While echoes laugh and trails unveil.

Unseen Connections

The squirrel scurries, oh what a tease,
Raiding the garden with utmost ease.
The flowers giggle, they can't be shy,
   As the sun winks a golden eye.

Through the fence, a friendly bark,
The dog next door joins in the lark.
With every nod, the world does spin,
   In this garden, chaos breeds a grin.

Ghosts of Longing

In the attic, a chair creaks,
A ghost with a soft peak,
Lost socks and missing shoes,
Come forth with jolly blues.

They dance in their own twist,
With every chance they insist,
To munch on the crumbs we leave,
In the corners, they believe.

Voices from the Other Side

A phone rings, but it's not yours,
It chimes from beneath the floors,
"Hey, are you free for a chat?"
A phantom voice? Imagine that!

With jokes of old they delight,
Giggling through the dead of night,
Tales of how they drowned in cake,
Making buns, for goodness' sake!

Secrets Linger in Moonlight

Under the light of glowing beams,
Cats hold council, plotting schemes,
With whiskers twitching in delight,
They share secrets of the night.

A shadow leaps, a toy is tossed,
The laughter echoes, never lost,
Under the moon's playful glance,
They swirl in a goofy dance.

Hidden Heartbeats

A thump from behind the wall,
Is that a heartbeat? Could it call?
A rumor that a house is alive,
Unseen friends, oh they contrive!

They tickle the chairs, make them sway,
In a game of hide and play,
With giggles muffled, they roam free,
Is that laughter, or just me?

Shades of the Unspoken

In the night, the curtains sway,
Mice in slippers do ballet.
The cat's staring, already wise,
Plotting schemes of feline spies.

Outside shadows dance with glee,
A squirrel's acorn jubilee.
The dog's barking, thinks he's grand,
While owls hoot plans, a wild band.

Chairs creak softly, a ghostly tease,
As ghosts sip tea among the trees.
Cakes laid out for a sweet delight,
Served by bats who love the night.

Hearts are bouncing, laughter shared,
Dreams are formed, but none prepared.
What secrets hide, they slyly cheep,
As moonlight winks and shadows creep.

The Language of Silence

Two cats argue, tails held high,
The dog just sits, with a sleepy sigh.
A bird outside chirps in delight,
While the goldfish swims, not a care in sight.

Neighbors yell, yet no one hears,
Laughter spills amid the jeers.
Chairs creak softly, as if in jest,
The clock ticks on, without a quest.

Shadows Speak Softly

In the night, the shadows dance,
A broomstick's flight? A funny chance!
They tiptoe 'round with glee and pride,
As the moon just chuckles, glowing wide.

A cat wearing socks, what a sight!
Sprinting away in the pale moonlight.
The lamp flickers with mischievous cheer,
While laughter echoes, ever near.

Muffled Thoughts of Light

A toast at dawn with toast so bright,
Jams and jellies in a playful fight.
Butterflies giggle in the warm sun,
While breakfast debates who's most fun.

A pancake flips, makes its escape,
Landing in syrup, a rules-free shape.
Spoons are dancing, forks are too,
In this kitchen, chaos brews.

Echoes of Yesterday

Old socks chat in the laundry bin,
Arguing 'bout where they've been.
A shirt grumbles, 'Toss me high!'
While pants just giggle, 'Give it a try!'

Memories dart like fireflies at play,
Painting the night in their quirky way.
The fabric hums a tune of cheer,
As yesterday's tales dance near.

In the Stillness of the Moment

A cat in pajamas plays with a shoe,
The dog thinks it's dinner, oh what a view!
Mice in the cupboard, a wild little spree,
Join the fun party, oh come, do agree!

Birds wear tiny hats, chirping the song,
While squirrels in tuxedos dance to the throng.
The moon gives a wink, stars chuckle with glee,
It's a raucous affair, come on, can't you see?

Beyond the Reflection

A mirror declares, 'I'm feeling quite grand!'
While a sock on the floor raises its hand.
Brooms break into dance, they duet with the mop,
The fridge hums a tune, makes all the cans bop!

A gnome on the shelf tips his hat to the night,
As spoons on the table take off in mid-flight.
The lamp laughs so hard, the shade starts to shake,
It's a shindig of joy, a wonderful wake!

Glistening Between Silence

The clock starts to tick with a silly old grin,
It chimes out a joke; let the fun now begin!
The curtains are giggling, swaying to and fro,
As chairs join the dance, putting on quite a show!

A sandwich complains of being devoured,
While forks clash in battle, oh how they're empowered!
Salt and pepper shakers trade jokes on the side,
As laughter erupts, no one can abide!

A Tapestry of Silent Secrets

Inky shadows plot with a flicker of light,
While vases converse of the floral delight.
Chairs play musical chairs, so bold and so bright,
As laughter spills forth in the soft, quiet night.

A lonely old sock starts a comedy book,
With punchlines that leave even a cactus shook!
The carpet rolls over, embracing the fun,
In this whimsical realm, there's no need to run!

Lurking in the Calm

In the hush of night, a snicker breaks,
Cats in capes plotting, oh what pranks!
A shadow darts, a giggle flee,
Squirrels dressed as thieves in jubilee.

Under the moon, the mirthful chase,
To steal the acorn, what a race!
They tumble and roll, a furry delight,
As laughter echoes through the night.

Hopes Entwined in Silence

Beneath the stars, a dance unfolds,
A chorus of critters, sweet and bold.
The hedgehogs whisper, 'What's the plan?'
While rabbits plot to steal the span.

With twinkling eyes, they take their stand,
A team of misfits in this wonderland.
Each leap and bound, a cunning feat,
As giggles burst in rhythmic beat.

Chasing Ghosts at Twilight

In twilight's glow, the laughter plays,
As shadows loom in mysterious ways.
A broomstick flies, a witch in flight,
Chasing dreams, oh, what a sight!

The pumpkin rolls, and spirits cheer,
All the while, we toast with beer!
A crispy breeze and joyful shrieks,
As ghostly giggles fill the peaks.

Secrets Reveal Themselves at Dusk

At dusk's embrace, the stories breed,
The wise old owl begins to lead.
With knowing eyes, it peeks and grins,
As crickets play, the fun begins.

Underneath the gnarled tree's bow,
The secrets spill, oh tell me how!
A tale of socks that wandered far,
And pajamas lost in the bizarre.

The Gap of Quietude

A cat in slippers, oh what a sight,
Prowling for snacks in the pale moonlight.
The fridge door creaks, a subtle debate,
Is it worth the risk for that late-night plate?

Laughter erupts as the spoon takes a dive,
Spaghetti noodles trying to come alive.
The dog's baffled gaze, a popcorn explosion,
All in the silence, a comical fusion.

Chasing the Faintest Sound

In a cozy corner, a chair starts to squeak,
"Is that a ghost?" we hear someone speak.
With a blanket as armor, we creep down the hall,
Ready to battle, or maybe just stall.

A shadow appears, it's just the old broom,
Bouncing around like it's ready to zoom.
Giggling softly at the antics within,
Quiet can be daring, and it sure is a win!

Sublime Sounds of Solitude

Amid the stillness, a hiccup unfolds,
Is it a secret or simply too bold?
Tick-tock the clock, it bursts into song,
A rhythm of quiet, yet never feels wrong.

The chair chats with crayons, the curtains agree,
As a lone poppy pot plants gossip with glee.
In the world of silence, delightfully shy,
Each giggle's a whisper, oh my, oh my!

Whispers That Never Were

A toaster chuckles, a kettle sings loud,
The vacuum's a dancer, drawing a crowd.
As socks organize a silent parade,
Who knew a home could be such a charade?

Bottles are grinning, the dishes conspire,
While brooms keep swaying, lost in their choir.
In the theater of quiet, laughter ignites,
The silliness crackles, oh what a delight!

Patterns of Unspoken Words

In the silence, secrets dance,
Laughter trapped, a jolly chance.
Chitter-chatter of the night,
Echoes of a playful light.

Behind the glass, a silly face,
Peeking out, a sneaky trace.
Giggling shadows, twinkling eyes,
Crafting mischief in disguise.

A dog barks at the moon's delight,
While cats plot in the pale moonlight.
Chasing dreams on a sleepy street,
Collecting tales with wobbly feet.

Gossip floats, a fluffy cloud,
Amongst the laughter, a wee bit loud.
Words unspoken, yet so clear,
In the jest, we find our cheer.

The Language of Stillness

Eyes twinkling in the dark,
Quiet giggles leave their mark.
With a nod, the tale unfolds,
Crafted whispers, sweet and bold.

A cat pounces, a shadow flies,
Creating chaos, no surprise.
Silent comedy, splatters of fun,
In the stillness, we've just begun.

Two lovers lean, their faces near,
But the squirrel steals the stage, oh dear.
A frolicsome plot under the stars,
In the stillness, here we are.

Smart remarks behind the pane,
Outside rain and inside bane.
In the calm, we find the flare,
In silence, jokes hang in the air.

Veiled Memories in the Moonlight

Moonbeams twirl like whispers sweet,
Bringing back folks on their feet.
A lantern flickers, a shadow prances,
In soft glow, the laughter dances.

Forgotten tales pop into view,
Adventures shared by me and you.
The ghost of giggles floats around,
In echoes of joy, our hearts are found.

Bewitching schemes in moonlit bloom,
Mischief lurks within the room.
Every glance, a jolly jest,
In veiled memories, we are blessed.

Old stories play like silly tunes,
Beneath the sway of lazy moons.
Cheeky mishaps turn our heads,
In memories, laughter spreads.

Intrigues in the Gloom

Shadows stretch, a plot in mind,
Under the haze, laughter entwined.
Footsteps tread on secrets low,
In the gloom, the tales overflow.

A creak, a laugh, a sudden dash,
Plans unravel in a funny flash.
What's hidden wriggles out to play,
In the intrigue, night turns to day.

With a wink, the games begin,
Comedy hides where none have been.
A misplaced cat, a runaway shoe,
In the gloom, we baffle the crew.

Beneath the surface, chuckles bloom,
Turning the dark into a room.
In every corner, fun abounds,
In the intrigue, joy resounds.

Tales of the Invisible

There's a ghost in my closet, so bold,
It sneezes out loud, but never gets cold.
Wearing my socks and my old winter hat,
It dances all night, imagine that!

When I peek in the fridge, what do I see?
A pickle and mustard hold hands with glee.
A sandwich telling a joke to some cheese,
The ketchup just giggles, it's hard to believe!

Secrets in the Shadows

In the corner where shadows play tricks,
A broom makes a friend with two dancing sticks.
They spin and they twirl without any care,
While the dust bunnies laugh at their flair.

The cat winks at me with a sly little grin,
As the chair starts to sway, oh what a sin!
They're planning a party, I'm sure it's grand,
With popcorn and cookies all made by hand!

Echoes of the Night

The moonlight tickles the tops of the trees,
Crickets are whispering, if you hear, please!
A frog takes the stage, it's his big debut,
With a croak like a trumpet, he's here for you!

A raccoon walks in with a mask on his face,
He's the sneaky bandit of this wild space.
Stealing the snacks from beneath the old bench,
While a firefly winks and calls him unhinged!

Murmurs in the Breeze

The wind brings giggles from friends far away,
I swear I can hear them, they're here to stay.
The daisies are gossiping under the sun,
"Oh my, look at him, he's trying to run!"

A butterfly lands, wearing bright little shoes,
He spins through the air, oh what a fun cruise!
While the clouds all chuckle, they puff up with pride,
As the sun joins the laugh, casting smiles worldwide!

Riddles of the Heart

A tickle in the chest, so bright,
Silly thoughts take off in flight.
Bunnies hop and dance with glee,
What's the secret? Come and see!

With cupcakes rolling down the lane,
Laughter bursts like drops of rain.
Is it magic, is it fate?
Or just a date with chocolate cake?

Unraveled Patterns of Noise

A sock that sings, a shoe that squeaks,
The world is full of silly peaks.
When teacups chatter late at night,
They share their dreams till morning light.

The clocks engage in merry fights,
Ticking tunes, in strange delights.
The kettle joins with true intent,
To whistle songs of discontent.

Resonance of a Hidden Tune

A cat in boots, with jazzy flair,
Tap dances while pretending to care.
With every scratch upon the floor,
It plays a tune we can't ignore.

The goldfish swims to bongo beats,
Their fins are dancing little treats.
Who knew the pond had such a flair?
A concert filled with fishy air!

Murmurs of Time Unfolding

The wall clocks giggle as they swing,
Each tick a joke, each tock a fling.
They whisper tales of days gone past,
With punchlines that will always last.

The curtains sway in happy glee,
Like dancers at a jubilee.
They know the secrets of each day,
And share them in a quirky way.

Flickers of Hope

In the night, the shadows dance,
A cat in boots took a chance.
It stumbles over a shoe,
Laughing loud, what a view!

The clock strikes with a silly chime,
As squirrels plot, they're up to their crime.
The neighbor's hat takes a flight,
Oh, what a comical sight!

With beams of light from the moon,
The garden gnomes hum a tune.
Tickling each flower's face,
In this whimsical, joyous space.

Laughter echoes through the air,
As hedgehogs attempt a dare.
They trip and roll, what a scene,
A show like this, it's serene!

Eclipsed Conversations

The stars gossip with the trees,
While giggling clowns float with ease.
A mouse in a tux joins the fun,
Whispering tales 'til the night is done.

The telephone pole can't hear a thing,
As frogs debate on a single swing.
They croak their tales with grand delight,
In this raucous, jovial night.

A raccoon juggles shiny spoons,
As owls hoot strange, quirky tunes.
With a wink, they share their secrets,
Underneath the twinkling beets.

Bananas slip, a grand surprise,
As daisies salute the disguised.
With laughter soft as a feather,
They gather for tea, all together.

Solitary Serenades

A lone giraffe sings a song,
The crickets dance, they sing along.
With each note, the daisies sway,
In a quirky, funny ballet.

The moon winks with a cheeky grin,
As fireflies twirl, they spin and spin.
A snail plays the tiny guitar,
What a tune from afar!

Sipping tea, the hedgehogs discuss,
Why pandas prefer the bus.
In their tales, chuckles arise,
Oh, the laughter never dies!

An ant recites poems of cheese,
While leaves flutter in the breeze.
With every rhyme, the world feels lighter,
In humor, hearts grow brighter.

Bated Breath Beneath the Stars

The cosmos giggles at our games,
As frogs play tag and call out names.
A rabbit prances with flair,
Chasing dreams without a care.

Underneath the shimmering night,
The owls hoot in sheer delight.
"Who's there?" asks a curious bee,
While dandelions sway carefree.

With a telescope pointed to the sky,
The raccoon claims, "I can fly!"
As wishes tumble down like rain,
Every star's a playful gain.

Eager whispers blend with the breeze,
The world in mischief, just to tease.
Each twinkle a giggle, each sigh a jest,
Under starlit antics, we feel blessed.

Glances Through the Curtains

Peeking out with eyes so wide,
Curiosity, my secret guide.
Neighbors dance with wild delight,
Who knew Tuesday could be so bright?

A dog on a skateboard, such a sight!
Chasing cats with all his might.
Laughing hard from our little spot,
Who knew our street was such a lot?

Overheard in the Midnight Hour

Late at night, the secrets sway,
A raccoon sings, who's next to play?
The couple fights about the socks,
While roaches dance on kitchen clocks.

The toaster pops, a toast to the dawn,
As midnight jokes push yawns along.
What's cooking in the bubbling pot?
Midnight snacks are always hot!

Softened Truths in the Dark

Whispers float like cream on tea,
Dog wants cake, I can see.
The cat's plotting a surprise,
Catching mice in evening guise.

Children giggle through the walls,
Pretend they're knights with shiny balls.
A hidden stash of candy bars,
While parents fight for secret jars.

Whispers of the Unseen

Bubbles float in a bath of cheer,
Rubber ducks have quite the fear.
Behind the glass, the night unfolds,
With tales of silliness never told.

The wind seems to sway, soft and light,
As shadows pirouette in the night.
Old tomes giggle on the shelf,
As if they know themselves so well.

Secrets in the Shadows

In a cozy nook, a cat's keen gaze,
Spying on the world with curious ways.
The dog barks loud, a squirrel takes flight,
Unraveling secrets in the calm of night.

A grumpy old man shakes his fist at the stars,
Yelling at creatures, from cats to guitars.
Under the moon, the garden does dance,
Both frog and rabbit seem caught in a trance.

The neighbor with cookies, oh what delight,
Lurks with a plate, trying not to bite.
As laughter erupts from the open door,
These silly secrets make spirits soar.

From the shadows, a giggle breaks free,
A garden of mischief, as wild as can be.
In the hush of dusk, with shadows that tease,
Life's playful riddles float with the breeze.

Echoes of the Night

The moon leans close to hear a few tales,
Of raccoons debating their nighttime trails.
With a spoon and a hat, they strategize well,
In this secret society, they laugh and dwell.

Crickets play symphonies to woo the moon,
While fireflies twirl like a tiny balloon.
A bounce and a hop, a light-hearted jest,
Every bug in the grass feels truly blessed.

A loud thud echoes, what could it be?
A gopher who startled, can't climb a tree.
They all burst out giggling, it's quite the sight,
In this madcap circus, all feels just right.

So the night rolls on, with echoes of cheer,
As antics unfold, the puzzles are clear.
In this whimsical shadow, joy takes its flight,
Every moment a treasure in the thick of night.

Murmurs Beyond the Glass

Behind the pane, with a curious gaze,
A gnome and a fairy concoct silly plays.
With a wink and a nudge, they sneak through the light,
Playing hopscotch with shadows that dance in the night.

A dog finds a bone; was it left there on cue?
Chasing his tail, he thinks it's brand new.
There's a giggle from flowers, a chuckle from leaves,
As they plot little pranks on those who believe.

The insect parade holds a splendid show,
With ants in a line, all ready to go.
A grasshopper leaps, and the crowd starts to cheer,
In this mischievous world, laughter is near.

As the moon dips low, the night blooms with laughter,
Every room is alive with their playful banter.
In this cheeky tableau, curiosity sows,
A world that is bursting with mirth as it grows.

Tales in the Twilight

As twilight descends, the air fills with giggles,
Toads gather 'round for their charming riddles.
A wise old owl hoots, 'What's green and can sing?'
All the trees shiver, waiting for spring.

The squirrels begin their late-night skit,
Practicing dance moves, oh, aren't they a hit!
Each flip and each twirl, a comic routine,
As shadows applaud, the scene is serene.

A fairy spills secrets from under the moon,
While a hedgehog hums an old, happy tune.
They swap funny tales of wandering cats,
Creating a saga of chattering bats.

So the night softly wraps all in its charm,
With a blanket of humor that keeps us all warm.
In the laughter-filled air, we find pure delight,
As we bask in the tales that glow in the night.

The Curtain's Secret

A sneaky cat with a curious gleam,
Lurks by the fabric, plotting a scheme.
Birds passing by, tease with a chirp,
While the curtain trembles, ready to burp!

Neighbors peek in, eyes wide with glee,
What's behind there? Is it just me?
With a sudden rustle and a soft little sound,
The mystery thickens, no answers found.

A sock with spots? A hat with flair?
This window's a stage for the odd and rare!
Under the sun or under the moon,
The antics unfold, a delightful cartoon.

As laughter erupts and a dog takes a bow,
The curtain reveals all, oh who knew how?
Life's little secrets dance in the light,
Through a window of mischief, pure joy in sight.

Undercurrents of Desire

Behind the glass, a couple does sway,
Flirting with shadows that dance and play.
With sips of tea and sweet little sighs,
They steal glances, wearing love-struck eyes.

A toast to the rain, as laughter erupts,
Their dog in the corner, huffing and chuffed.
With each playful tease, a wink and a grin,
The world outside fades, let the fun begin!

The mailman strolls by, curious to see,
What's brewing inside, oh, what could it be?
A waltz in the kitchen, a tango at dusk,
Even the fridge seems to hum with a trust.

As crumbs drift away like secrets on air,
The window holds tales that none can prepare.
Love's little antics, amusingly sly,
Under the gaze of the curious sky.

Intimate Inklings

A note on the sill, penned with delight,
Scribbles of dreams, oh what a sight!
A chorus of giggles leaks out like a breeze,
While the curtains jump, teasing the trees.

The neighbor's cat winks, perched on the ledge,
Wants in on the fun, makes a bold pledge.
Feathers and papers take flight in the room,
A whirlwind of chaos—oh, how it can zoom!

A mystery written in sweet little marks,
Shouting of plans, and secret remarks.
For behind every pane, a comic surprise,
With laughter that sparkles, and joyful goodbyes.

As night draws near, the stories align,
In the glow of a lamp, both silly and fine.
Every glance, every jest, shines bright as a star,
In the world of small moments, we're never too far.

Mysterious Murmurs at Midnight

In the dead of the night, with a soft little squeak,
The curtain unfurls, and the shadows speak.
A raccoon peeks in, with a twitch of his nose,
Looking for snacks, as the mischief grows.

Socks flying high, a tango of bliss,
Two toddlers giggle, plotting their miss.
A game of hide and seek wends through the room,
While the moon joins in, casting silvery gloom.

A kettle will whistle, a prank in its song,
Only to find out a teacup's gone wrong.
With giggles and hiccups, the echoes ring clear,
What stories unfold in the midnight cheer?

For behind that glass, with a murmur and laugh,
The world takes a bow, in a comical half.
So laugh with the night, let the chaos embark,
In the silent serenade, life makes its mark.

A Symphony of Quietude

In the silence, I hear a tune,
A sock on a cat, oh what a boon.
The fridge hums a melody so sweet,
While the goldfish plays its silent beat.

The clock ticks with laughter galore,
Each second it tells, it's hard to ignore.
Silly echoes dance in my ear,
As the house makes mischief, bringing cheer.

With kittens performing their acrobatic play,
And the dog dreaming dreams of a savory tray.
I swear there's a rhythm in the oven's roar,
As the popcorn pops, begging for more!

In this quiet space, joy takes the floor,
Where even the curtains conspire to snore.
Music of stillness, utterly round,
In the corners of calm, pure laughter is found.

The Unsaid

Behind closed doors, secrets dance,
A rubber chicken in a silly prance.
The echo of giggles, a muffled cheer,
While nobody knows who's really here.

An invisible game of peek-a-boo,
The shadow greets me, what's it up to?
Bubbles in soap, they drift and sway,
Like a tickle fight that won't go away.

Old Stirling the cat, he's on a quest,
To claim every nap as his very best.
The plant shakes with laughter, a windy tease,
As the curtains flap in a silly breeze.

Chairs whisper tales of past affairs,
With spaghetti strands in their tangled snares.
While laughter erupts in the oddest of places,
Where silence once lived, there are now funny faces.

Ghostly Gazes from Afar

In potted plants, shadows take flight,
As they plot their mischief all through the night.
I see one smile, it's wearing a hat,
Perhaps it's just Bertie, my enchanted cat.

The wallpaper fidgets, it winks at me,
While spoons giggle softly, as if to agree.
Without a giggle, they rustle and sway,
Turning my living room into a cabaret.

Invisible friends play in the light,
A dance of donuts, oh what a sight!
A poltergeist skips in mismatched shoes,
While the fridge gives me unsolicited news.

With every creak, there's an anecdote told,
As clock hands bounce like marbles of gold.
In this room of fun, glee rides the tail,
Of ghostly gazes and silly tales.

In the Curve of a Dusk

As evening yet grins with a crazy glow,
Chickens in tutus begin their show.
With pirouettes under the moon's wide grin,
Our garden becomes a theatrical spin.

Fireflies audition, oh what a light!
While the toad croaks his baritone fright.
The daisies giggle, their petals all tease,
At the antics that dance on the fluttering breeze.

In the nook of twilight, a wonderful sight,
The gnomes are at play, what sheer delight!
With each little wink from the stars up above,
The night swells with laughter, the world full of love.

Balloons from nowhere float past the trees,
As crickets compose their own symphonies.
Every rustle and laugh fills the air with cheer,
As dusk ushers in fun, making worries disappear.

Hushed Voices at Dusk

Silly secrets shared at night,
Cats eavesdropping in delight.
Mice giggle, a chirp and dance,
Outside the glow of firefly chance.

Beneath the stars, a comic scene,
Balloons squeak, or so it seems.
A squirrel wearing mismatched socks,
Thinks it's fashion—what a shock!

Neighbors argue, but wait, oh dear,
Is that a carrot stuck in here?
Laughter echoed 'neath the moon,
As raccoons sing the silly tune.

The night air thick with playful jest,
In our world, we're simply blessed.
Unseen but felt, the joy we find,
With chuckles dancing on the mind.

Soft Sounds of Solitude

Listen close, what do you hear?
A sock puppet dropping a sneer.
The clock chuckles, ticks just right,
As gnomes dance in the pale moonlight.

Chairs creak like they're in a play,
They've got their own things to say.
A turtle grumbles, "I'm not slow!,"
While hiring crickets in a show.

Soft sighs from the fridge, how odd,
As pickles start to groan and prod.
A blender hums a tune so fine,
Fruits in a whirl for punch divine!

Each corner holds a subtle hum,
Laughter brewing, here it comes!
In the quiet, fun does bloom,
A solo party in the room.

Lurking Beneath the Surface

In the garden, fears collide,
A squirrel plotting, oh what pride!
With acorns stacked in a tall tower,
He's planning for the nutty hour!

Underneath the leafy green,
A worm stirs, unseen, so keen.
He wriggles with a twinkling eye,
Singing songs of sweet supply!

Beneath the deck, what do I see?
A frog disguised as a bumblebee!
Hopping about with a budding croak,
Mistaken identity—what a joke!

With shadows stretching long and wide,
Comedic chaos they can't abide.
Rooted deep, the giggles grow,
Life beneath, a funny show.

Unseen Conversations

In the kitchen, pots conspire,
The kettle grumbles, "I'm on fire!"
While spoons chatter, forks dispute,
The bread sings a doughy flute.

Behind the curtain, voices hum,
Jars of jelly start to drum.
A pickle pipes in, loud and brash,
While biscuits whisper—what a clash!

The floorboards creak, they call for fun,
"Let's party, let's run!" Just begun!
The cookies sigh, "We're feeling crummy,"
As marshmallows bounce, oh so gummy!

Unnoticed tales of joy unfold,
In the quiet, laughter bold.
A mystery wrapped in jolly cheer,
Unseen chats that draw us near.

The Silence Between Us

In shadows we sit, bare feet on the floor,
As we dodge the gossip from the neighbor next door.
Your eyebrows lift high when the cat starts to leap,
We share a fine chuckle; secrets we keep.

The clock strikes a hour, but we linger to chat,
About wild assumptions, like where is that cat?
You laugh 'til you snort over tales of old,
While I pretend to listen, being quite bold.

The silence is thick, like jelly on toast,
Both hoping for nonsense, we tease and we boast.
Yet over the giggles, a mystery gleams,
What secrets lie hidden behind our bright dreams?

A knock at the door; oh no, is it fate?
Who could it be? Should we seal that escape?
We silently panic, like kids caught in pranks,
But we're just two fools sharing laughs at the banks.

Soft Footfalls on the Glass

The rain pitter-patters, a soft little dance,
And giggles escape us, lost in a trance.
Your dog does a twirl on the couch like a star,
While the outside world's chaos feels quite far.

The neighbors are peeking, my, what a show!
Two shadows of silliness, covering woe.
With socks on our heads and markers in hand,
We sketch out our lives, dream plots so grand.

Oh, how we chuckle at what they might think,
As we preserve our tales, like ink in the pink.
The world beyond glass becomes wild and absurd,
We whisper sweet secrets without saying a word.

But every soft footfall sends quakes through our fun,
A dance of euphoria, two clowns on the run.
Yet tales stick like gum on the soles of our shoes,
Creating a laughter that nobody can lose.

Unspoken Conversations

What's better than silence? A grin or a wink,
As we spy on the world through the bubbles of drink.
Your smirk says it all, without needing to speak,
While I twirl my spaghetti, sheer chaos, so chic.

Our eyes do the talking, the silliness flows,
Like fumbles with forks or a sneeze that just grows.
From secret conspiracies over fish on the floor,
To fits of the giggles; oh, please, would you snore?

We play peekaboo games with the light through the shade,

As we chuckle at life, these moments we've made.
Unspoken connections, like threads made of lace,
A patchwork of laughter we can't help but embrace.

So here's to the exchanges that knock on the glass,
To the mischief we spark, and the moments that pass.
For though words may be few, the humor runs deep,
In the quiet of knowing, our secrets we keep.

Veiled Voices at Dusk

As shadows grow longer and light starts to fade,
We gather our thoughts in a strange masquerade.
Your side-eye belongs in a circus, so wild,
As I clutch at my stomach, oh, how I've reviled!

The moon sneaks a peek through the cracks of the frame,
While we mime for the world, like it's all just a game.
Shh! Listen closely, you've got quite the knack,
For crafting our gags, like the wind at our back.

Sudden thoughts bubble like gum on the floor,
Each giggle a treasure, oh, we just want more!
The air fills with stories that spin and take flight,
As dusk turns to laughter; oh, what a delight!

Though the neighbors may wonder, we'll just carry on,
Two sprites turning twilight into our own dawn.
With veils made of giggles, we wrap up our night,
In the glow of our antics, everything's bright.

Secrets Veiled in Silence

In corners crouch the silly thoughts,
Of who forgot to wash the socks.
A cat meows, pretending to plot,
While the dog secretly stalks the blocks.

The clock ticks on, a sneaky sound,
Like laughter hiding in the night.
Each creak of floorboards spins around,
As shadows dance until the light.

With giggles masked by bedtime tales,
The secrets float on moonlit trails.
A sock's lost somewhere, who can tell?
The dog grins wide, oh what the hell!

Come morning light, the truth appears,
The socks unite, dismissing fears.
And laughter marks the new day's cheer,
As secrets veiled fade, disappear.

The Silent Song of Starlight

Above the rooftops, stars do wink,
They know the secrets, more than we think.
A squirrel sings, in nets of dreams,
While the moon rolls eyes, or so it seems.

The wind hums softly, secrets in tow,
Of cat escapades we'll never know.
It tickles trees, and tickles me,
Scoffing at rules, just wild and free.

Dandelions dance in playful glee,
As shadows tango, two or three.
Hearts in stitches, all quite all right,
With laughter threaded through the night.

So lift your cup to twinkling bliss,
In the silent song, a cosmic kiss.
Beneath the hush, the laughter flows,
The starlight knows what mischief grows.

Voids of Intimacy

In the space between our cheeky grins,
Lie tales of cats and fuzzy sins.
A sock that vanished, oh what a thrill,
Is hiding under the couch, so still.

Dare we peek in the pantry late?
Searching for sweets on a sneaky date.
Laughter erupts within those walls,
As secrets tumble, under bouncy balls.

Tickles of laughter fill the air,
In cozy shadows, we show we care.
A ticked-off goldfish swims with style,
Watching our antics with a fishy smile.

So here's to cuddles in stolen hours,
Moments that bloom like wildflowers.
In voids of intimacy, we dare,
To crack the jokes that hang in the air.

Hidden Lullabies

In the attic, where dust bunnies play,
Lies a treasure of giggles in the fray.
A moth takes flight, on a quest for more,
While shadows follow around the floor.

The clock whispers, 'Shh, tell no one!'
As cats chase tails, oh what fun.
Each little creak, a lullaby sweet,
Turns into chuckles beneath our feet.

The slip of a letter, the tip of a shoe,
Mischief awakens with every clue.
Sprite-like laughter spills from the eaves,
Gathering tales like autumn leaves.

As starlight bathes the home in glow,
We tiptoe softly, sharing the show.
With secrets tucked and joy in the air,
Hidden lullabies, a world we share.

Secrets of an Open Heart

A creaky door lets in a breeze,
While squirrels plot to steal from trees.
My heart sings loud, a silly tune,
As birds gossip 'neath the lazy moon.

Giggles of leaves in playful dance,
A toe-tapping rhythm, give fate a chance.
With every glance, a secret shared,
Nonsense sprinkles, none are spared.

The cat peers out with a single eye,
Dreams of fish that swim up high.
He knows the tales of sun and night,
And laughs at shadows that seem to bite.

As raindrops patter on the sill,
The world outside, a merry thrill.
In this chaos, my heart's set free,
Singing to all, just let it be!

Phantoms in the Breeze

A gust of wind with a playful grin,
Sneaks past the walls, let the fun begin.
I hear the laughter of ghosts so spry,
They twirl like leaves in the autumn sky.

Old hats thrown high in a bantering flight,
Flap and flutter, oh what a sight!
The garden gnomes all start to sway,
As secrets tumble in a strange ballet.

Laughter echoes from the bough,
What do the flowers whisper now?
Their colors burst, a cheeky show,
Blowing kisses without a bow.

Under the stars, mischief brews,
In this painted world, we chase the hues.
Each twinkle giggles, each cloud complies,
While moonlit giggles fill the skies.

The Stillness Between Words

A pause that's thick, like honey spread,
In the silence, laughter's fed.
I wink at shadows, give a nod,
They laugh back, oh what a squad!

Chirps and beeps, a joyous noise,
Even the trees have their toys.
Beneath the stillness, mischief waits,
In hushed tones, punchlines create fates.

A squeaky mouse with tales to share,
Winks at the cat, unaware of a scare.
In this dance of hush and hum,
Life wagged its tail, a jovial drum.

In each silence, jokes reside,
As the sun dips low, and shadows slide.
Here's to the laughter, soft yet bold,
In the stillness, happiness unfolds.

Whispers on the Edge of Night

As twilight casts its dreamy hue,
The world giggles in a silly view.
Stars nudge each other, playing a game,
While the moon chuckles, calling each name.

Clouds drift by with mischief in tow,
Juggling fireflies, putting on a show.
As laughter echoes from every nook,
Cats curl up, taking a look.

A tickling breeze, a soft caress,
Hints of secrets we want to guess.
Each cranny holds a tale to spin,
Even the crickets wear cheeky grins.

In the darkness, joy shines bright,
With each chuckle, we toast the night.
Let the world keep spinning, twist and twirl,
For laughter lingers in every swirl.

Notes from a Distant Realm

A poodle with a monocle, so refined,
Dances in the moonlight, quite unconfined.
Cats hold a council, plotting a prank,
Balloon laughter echoes, filling their bank.

Mice in tuxedos, sipping on tea,
Debate if the clock ticked or just agreed.
Ghosts play chess with shadows and beams,
Stirring the night with their dreamy schemes.

Tea bags gossiping, snickering loud,
While kitchen spices form a merry crowd.
Toasters sing opera, bread in a trance,
Jam jars rumba, it's a wobbly dance.

In corners where giggles seem to abound,
Socks carry tales that cannot be found.
The clock strikes laughter, a giggling chime,
Counting the moments, the joy, and the grime.

Shadows Cradling Secrets

A sneaky raccoon wears shades at night,
Dodging the moonbeams with comical fright.
Kittens play poker with chips made of cheese,
As fireflies flicker, trying to tease.

A squirrel with acorns is quite the big shot,
Betting on adventures that hit the right spot.
The owls are snoozing, their wisdom on pause,
While crickets recite their hilarious laws.

Peppers are plotting a spicy delight,
They giggle and wiggle in the warm neon light.
The cupboards are dancing, a faint jig and sway,
To melodies only the curtains can play.

Laughter travels like breadcrumbs in air,
Tickling the dust, without a care.
And under the table, what do we find?
Jellybeans laughing, in colors entwined.

Faint Calls from the Unknown

A chair hums softly, it knows the best jokes,
While old dusty books join in with some pokes.
The curtains are chuckling, swaying in glee,
Welcoming shadows, playing hide and seek.

Balloons float by, with a wink and a grin,
Advertising fun that just wouldn't begin.
Teapots break dance, revving up for a spill,
While butter's slipping smoothly, what a thrill!

Pans in the kitchen perform a duet,
Banging and crashing, the best that we'll get.
Remote controls wonder why they're misplaced,
Amidst laughter that dances all over the space.

Tripping on giggles, the night takes its cue,
As even the dust bunnies join in the view.
With wrapped-up joy lighting up every nook,
The magic still lingers, like a well-read book.

The Quiet Between Us

The clock is a gossip, tick-tocking away,
Making sure no secret can ever stay.
A lollipop whispers of flavors untold,
While gummy bears giggle, feeling quite bold.

Waffle irons sing, releasing a tune,
In a kitchen where chaos welcomes the moon.
Marshmallows dance, their fluffiness grand,
As pancakes rise up, they take a firm stand.

Chairs crack a joke about their worn-out legs,
While spoons tell tales of oh-so-busy pegs.
The fridge hums softly, a lullaby sweet,
Scoops of ice cream join in for the feat.

In the spaces between, there's laughter and cheer,
Where cutlery's banter rings clear as a bell.
In moments so subtle, joy hides and calls,
Glancing through fragments in innocent halls.

The Sound of Hidden Lives

In shadows cast by dimming light,
A cat debates if it should fight.
The dog is snoring like a train,
While birds outside plot their insane.

A mouse plays tag with his own tail,
As owls above begin to rail.
The fridge hums secrets, soft and sweet,
While chairs conspire beneath our feet.

The goldfish gestures, quite the show,
As curtains dance to winds that blow.
A squirrel wriggles in despair,
While everyone pretends not to care.

And laughter bubbles, sheer delight,
From hidden rooms that party all night.
In silence, chaos reigns supreme,
Where every nook's a lively dream.

Echoes of Forgotten Dreams

A sock lies lost beneath the bed,
Convinced it's plotting, dreams of dread.
The clock ticks tales of yore and woe,
While teacups crackle with laughter's glow.

The toaster pops like it has news,
'Get your own toast!' it seems to muse.
The vacuum hums its silly tune,
As curtains wince and start to swoon.

Each shadow flails in comic grace,
As broomsticks weave a wacky race.
Cheeky spiders spin yarns so bold,
In alleys where all secrets unfold.

The echoes dance, with joy they prance,
For every room's a chance to chance.
And in the hush, a giggle swells,
For forgotten dreams know how to tell.

Behind the Shelter of Silence

The couch expands, a perfect lair,
Where snacks conspire without a care.
The lampshade's plotting quite the jest,
While floors rattle, 'We need a rest!'

The coffee pot spills beans like tea,
'Come join the mishap,' it seems to plea.
Each window grins a sly little grin,
As socks brigade for a kooky win.

The pet rock throws a wild party,
With dust bunnies acting quite farty.
The wallpaper peels back a grin,
As walls hum tales of silent sin.

In stillness, mischief grows so bold,
A masquerade of laughter told.
Each secret kept in quiet schemes,
Brews lovely chaos in funny dreams.

Stories That Refuse to Fade

Old brooms recount their flying days,
While pots and pans join in the play.
The library murmurs tales once spun,
Of heroes lost and races run.

An umbrella frets of rainy woes,
While mirrored reflections play peek-a-boo shows.
The rug rolls out with crafty schemes,
To weave together all our dreams.

Chairs are grumpy, claiming their space,
While shadows fall with a zebra's grace.
Plates reminisce of meals well shared,
As empty bowls claim no one dared.

In laughter's arms, the stories rise,
Through dusty nooks and playful sighs.
For nothing lost is ever dead,
In every heart lies what's been said.

www.ingramcontent.com/pod-product-compliance
Lightning Source LLC
Chambersburg PA
CBHW062112280426
43661CB00086B/560